Grammar, Usage, & Mechanics

By the Editors of TIME FOR KIDS

Teacher Created Materials
PUBLISHING

TIME FOR KIDS®
Grammar, Usage, and Mechanics
Level 2
Copyright © 2005
Reprinted 2011
Time Inc.

TIME FOR KIDS and the Red Border Design are registered trademarks of Time Inc. All rights reserved. Developed in collaboration with *Exploring Writing* from Teacher Created Materials.

TIME FOR KIDS
Editorial Director: Keith Garton
Editor: Jonathan Rosenbloom
Project Editor: Mary McClellan,
    Baseline Development Group
Design Production: Jennifer Brown, Dinardo Design
Illustrator: Jackie Snider
Teacher Reviewers: Holly Albrecht, WI; Marian Evans, TX; Ryann Kelso, IL; Karen Lawson, OH; Christine Libeu, CA; Karen Mauro, NY; Julie Morgan, NE; Mary Paskvan, MN; Jeff Reed, PA; Jana Underwood, TX

Exploring Writing™
Copyright © 2005
Teacher Created Materials Publishing

Teacher Created Materials
Publisher: Rachelle Cracchiolo, M.S. Ed.
Editor-in-Chief: Sharon Coan, M.S. Ed.
Editorial Project Manager: Dona Herweck Rice

All rights reserved. No part of this book may be reproduced in any form without express written permission from the publisher. No part of this publication may be transmitted, stored, or recorded in any form without written permission from the publisher.

ISBN: 978-1-7439-0127-4

Teacher Created
Materials Publishing
5301 Oceanus Drive
Huntington Beach, CA 92649
www.tcmpub.com

Photography Credits

Page 11: Burke/Triolo Productions/BrandXPictures; Page 15: Photodisc; Page 20: Comstock; Page 23: Brand X Pictures/Punchstock; Page 26: Comstock; Page 29: Index Open; Page 31: Ingram Publishing; Page 35: NASA; Page 36: Photodisc; Page 42: AP Wide World Photos; Page 47: Photodisc; Page 50: Photodisc; Page 54: U.S. Army Photo; Page 55: AP Wide World Photos; Page 58: Photodisc; Page 60: NASA

 For more writing practice: www.timeforkids.com/hh/writeideas

Grammar, Usage, & Mechanics

❶ Sentences
Sentences 1–2
Naming Parts of Sentences 3–4
Action Parts of Sentences 5–6

❷ Nouns
Nouns 7–8
Special Nouns 9–10
Plural Nouns 11–12
Special Plural Nouns 13–14

❸ Verbs
Verbs 15–16
Verbs That Tell About Now 17–18
Verbs That Tell About the Past 19–20
Special Verbs 21–22
Other Special Verbs 23–24
Contractions 25–26

❹ Adjectives

Adjectives 27–28
a, *an*, and *the* 29–30
Special Adjectives 31–32
Comparing with Adjectives 33–34

❺ Adverbs

Adverbs That Tell How 35–36
Adverbs That Tell When or Where 37–38

❻ Pronouns

Pronouns. 39–40
More Pronouns 41–42

❼ Possessives

Possessive Nouns 43–44
More Possessive Nouns 45–46
Possessive Pronouns 47–48

❽ Capitalization and Punctuation Guide

Days and Months 49–50
Abbreviations and Titles 51–52
Commas 53–54
Quotation Marks 55–56

❾ Usage Guide

Using *I* and *me* 57–58
Combining Sentences 59–60
Frequently Misspelled Words . . . . Inside back cover

Sentences

Name _____   Date _____

Sentences

A **sentence** tells a complete thought. There are four kinds of sentences. Every sentence begins with a capital letter.

A **telling sentence** tells something. It ends with a period.

It is fun to watch a parade**.**

A **question** asks something. It ends with a question mark.

Which float do you like best**?**

A **command** tells someone to do something. It usually ends with a period.

Clap for the girls holding the flags**.**

An **exclamation** shows strong feeling. It ends with an exclamation point.

That is the biggest balloon I have ever seen**!**

❶ Show What You Know

Write the correct end mark to finish each sentence.   . ? !

1. A band marches down the street _____

2. Listen to the music _____

3. Are the drums loud _____

4. This is the best parade ever _____

Grammar, Usage, and Mechanics—Level 2   **1**

Sentences

Name _____ Date _____

❷ Take It Up a Notch

Write different kinds of sentences to tell about the picture. Be sure to use the correct end mark for each sentence.

Telling Sentence _____

_____

Question _____

_____

Command _____

_____

Exclamation _____

_____

❸ On Your Own

Sentence Changes Write a short sentence. See if a partner can change your sentence into another kind. Take turns writing and changing sentences.

Question: Will you wear a hat? ➝ **Command:** Wear a hat.

Make your writing more interesting for readers by using at least two kinds of sentences.

Naming Parts of Sentences

Every sentence has a **naming part.**

The **naming part** of a sentence tells who or what the sentence is about.

Many animals live in the sea.

The fish swim in the salty water.

They move their fins back and forth.

Max watches a school of fish.

❶ Show What You Know

Draw a line under the naming part of each sentence.

1. The children play at the beach.
2. Liz floats on her back.
3. A little boat sails by.
4. Ben digs in the sand.
5. He makes a big castle.

Go on

Naming Parts of Sentences

Name _____ Date _____

❷ Take It Up a Notch

Fill in the naming part of each sentence. Use the words in the word box. Remember to begin the first word of each sentence with a capital letter.

| A crab | A shark | A seagull | A man | A plant |

1. _____ flies high above the sand.

2. _____ swims with fins.

3. _____ crawls slowly near the water.

4. _____ grows underwater.

5. _____ goes to the beach to swim.

❸ On Your Own

Sentence Puzzles Each person in a small group should write a telling sentence on a strip of paper. Cut the paper after the naming part of the sentence. Trade your naming part for someone else's naming part. Work together to see how many new sentences you can make!

TFK Tips for Writers

Help make your writing sound better by making sure that the naming parts of your sentences are clear. Try to change sentences that are not clear.

                Ana
Example: ~~She~~ trains seals. **She** teaches the seals tricks.

Action Parts of Sentences

Action Parts of Sentences

Every sentence has a naming part. Every sentence also has an action part. The **action part** of a sentence tells what happens.

Luis **planted seeds.**

The naming part of this sentence is Luis. The **action part** of this sentence is **planted seeds.**

Examples of Action Parts
Beans and carrots **grew.**
He **waters his garden every day.**
His plants **grow tall.**

❶ Show What You Know

Circle the action part of each sentence.

1. We walk behind the barn.
2. The farmer shows us her pumpkin patch.
3. She smiles.
4. My sister finds a big, round pumpkin.
5. I choose a small one.

Go on

Action Parts of Sentences

Name _____ Date _____

❷ Take It Up a Notch

Fill in the action part of each sentence. Use the words in the word box.

> **fall off the tree.   chases a squirrel.
> are putting apples into a basket.**

1. Sam and Charlie _____

2. Their puppy _____

3. Some apples _____

Proofreading Power!

Find four mistakes in this letter. Use proofreader's marks to fix them.

Dear Aunt Val,

   Our class planted a vegetable garden. our teacher gave us seeds? My friends put them into the ground When the plants are big, we will give the food to families who need it. come see our garden.

   Love,
   Matt

∧	Add
—	Take out
/	Make a lowercase letter
≡	Make a capital letter
⊙	Add a period

6   Grammar, Usage, and Mechanics—Level 2

Nouns

A **noun** names a person, a place, or a thing.

Person	One **hiker** climbed quickly.
Place	The **campground** is close.
Thing	Is your **backpack** heavy?

Person	The **camper** likes to hike.
Place	She went to the **forest** two days ago.
Thing	Her **tent** is green.

❶ Show What You Know

Draw a line under the noun in each sentence.

1. We are camping near a tree.
2. A lake is nearby.
3. Some birds sing sweetly.
4. We make a fire.
5. We study the map.

Go on

Nouns

Name _____   Date _____

❷ Take It Up a Notch
Circle the noun in each group.

1. small   trail   walked
2. looked   tired   boot
3. town   slowly   up
4. rocky   far   girl
5. sits   fire   pretty

❸ On Your Own

Three Kinds of Nouns Think of nine nouns. Try to think of three nouns from each group: person, place, and thing. Write each noun on a card. Shuffle your cards, and then trade with a friend. See how quickly you can sort your friend's words into the three groups.

 **TFK Tips for Writers**

Good writers use exact nouns to give readers a clear picture. Look at a story or a letter you are writing. See if you can change any nouns to make them more exact.

                    bee   daisy
Example: The ~~insect~~ landed on a ~~flower~~.

Special Nouns

Name _____ Date _____

Special Nouns

Some nouns name a special person, place, or thing.
Special nouns begin with capital letters.

Nouns	Special Nouns
girl	**M**aria
town	**B**uttonwood
street	**L**ake **S**treet
building	**R**obbins **S**chool
pet	**S**cout

❶ Show What You Know

Draw a line under the special nouns in each sentence.

1. There was once a king named Rich.

2. His castle was on Crown Street.

3. It was near a river in the city of Princeton.

4. The king's dog, Duke, was very smart.

5. At the Puppy Castle School, he learned many tricks.

Special Nouns

Name _____ Date _____

❷ Take It Up a Notch

Write a special noun from the box in each blank to finish the paragraph.

Happy School	Flapper	Benjamin
Market Street	Mars	Jessica

My friends and I are putting on a puppet show. It is about a boy named _____ and his sister named _____ . The children live in an apartment on _____ . During the week, they go to school at the _____ . On weekends, they take exciting trips with their talking bird named _____ . One day, they fly to _____ .

❸ On Your Own

Make-Believe Town Draw a picture of a make-believe town. Write special nouns to label the people, places, and things.

TFK Tips for Writers

Look for places in your writing where special nouns would make sentences clearer and give more exact information.

Example: The bus stops at the end of ~~the street~~. Lily Lane

Plural Nouns

Name _____ Date _____

Nouns can name one person, place, or thing.

Nouns can also name more than one person, place, or thing.

One	More Than One
One **boy** made pizza.	Two **boys** made pizza.

Add **s** to most nouns to name more than one.

Add **es** to nouns that end with **s, x, ch,** or **sh.**

One	More Than One
cake	cake**s**
bus	bus**es**
fox	fox**es**
bench	bench**es**
brush	brush**es**

❶ Show What You Know

Write the noun in each sentence that names more than one.

1. We help our parents at home. _____

2. I make some sandwiches for lunch. _____

3. My brothers wash the dirty dishes. _____

4. Pam and Joanna carry boxes. _____

5. Tia and Juanita sew dresses. _____

Go on

Plural Nouns

Name _____ Date _____

❷ Take It Up a Notch

Write the noun in each blank so that it names more than one. Add s or es.

There are many _____ to do on the ranch. Tali
                                           job

feeds hay to the _____ . Deon trims the
                             horse

_____ that grow beside the stable. Then he builds
     bush

fences to keep the _____ away. We all
                             fox

pick ripe _____ from the trees. Papa gives us
            peach

hugs and _____ when we are done!
           kiss

❸ On Your Own

What's My Word? Think of a noun that names more than one and ends with **s** or **es**. On a piece of paper, draw a blank for each letter in the word. Ask a partner to try to name the word by guessing one letter at a time. Fill in the correct letters as your partner guesses them.

TFK Tips for Writers

When you proofread your writing, check the spelling and endings of all the nouns that name more than one.

Special Plural Nouns

Name _____ Date _____

Special Plural Nouns

Some nouns change their spelling when they name more than one.

One	More Than One
child	two **children**
man	many **men**
woman	five **women**
foot	two **feet**
mouse	some **mice**

❶ Show What You Know

Circle the correct noun in ( ) to finish each sentence.

1. Jarel put warm boots on his (foots/feet).

2. He was going to the library with some (children/child).

3. Two (women/womans) helped them find books.

4. One book was about a few (man/men) who went to the moon.

5. Another book was about some talking (mouses/mice).

Go on

Plural Nouns

Name _____ Date _____

❷ Take It Up a Notch

Finish each sentence. Change and write the noun in red to mean more than one.

1. The _____ in Ms. Yi's class like to write.
   child

2. They send cards to _____ in the hospital.
   man

3. Pete wrote a report about white _____ .
   mouse

4. Eva's story about two _____ is silly.
   woman

5. The women have a dog that is six _____ tall!
   foot

Proofreading Power!

Find five mistakes on this poster. Use proofreader's marks to fix them.

Come to a book talk
on Monday at noon!

It's at the baker School on Elm street.

Hear ellen Lowd talk about her new

cookbook about healthy lunchiz.

All adults and childs are welcome!

∧	Add
—	Take out
/	Make a lowercase letter
≡	Make a capital letter
⊙	Add a period

14   Grammar, Usage, and Mechanics—Level 2   #10127 (iz98)

Verbs

A verb usually names an action.

The children **sit** outside.

They **listen** to the park ranger.

She **talks** about the bats in the cave.

The children **explore** the cave with the park ranger.

They **see** bats in the cave.

❶ Show What You Know

Draw a line under the verb in each sentence.

1. Bats sleep during the day.
2. They fly at night.
3. Most bats eat bugs.
4. Many bats live in caves.
5. Some bats hang from tree branches.

Grammar, Usage, and Mechanics—Level 2

Verbs

Name _____ Date _____

❷ Take It Up a Notch
Write the verb you see in each group.

1. animal   food   hunts   _____
2. sees   dark   inside   _____
3. sky   throw   high   _____
4. cliff   jumps   down   _____
5. chew   quietly   food   _____

❸ On Your Own

Verbs on Stage Play this game with a small group. One person thinks of a verb that names an action. That person acts out the verb without speaking. The others in the group try to guess the word. The person who guesses correctly thinks of the next action verb and acts it out.

jump

TFK Tips for Writers

Good writers use exact verbs to paint a clear word picture for their readers. Reread a paper you are writing to see if you can make any of the action verbs more exact.

　　　　　　　　traps
Example: The bat ~~gets~~ a bug with its wings.

Verbs That Tell About Now

A **verb** can tell about an action that is happening now.

Add **s** to a now verb that tells about one person, place, or thing.

> One boy **makes** a mask.
>
> He **cuts** out holes for the eyes.

Do not add **s** to a now verb that tells about more than one person, place, or thing.

> Two boys **make** masks.
>
> They **cut** out holes for the eyes.

❶ Show What You Know
Circle the correct verb in ( ) to finish each sentence.

1. Mrs. Morris (sew/sews) costumes for the play.
2. The children (learn/learns) their parts.
3. Sara (stand/stands) on the stage.
4. She (sing/sings) her song two times.
5. The bright lights (shine/shines) on her.

Verbs That Tell About Now

Name _____ Date _____

❷ Take It Up a Notch

Write a verb from the box to finish each sentence.

| chases | say | pulls | claps | hop |

1. Oscar _____ the curtain open.

2. The rabbits _____ their lines.

3. Then they _____ across the stage.

4. The farmer _____ them.

5. Mr. Foster _____ for the actors.

❸ On Your Own

Noun-Verb Match With a partner, write these verbs on cards: **hum, shout, dig, leap, swim.** Shuffle the verb cards and put them face down into a pile. Take turns pulling one card from the pile. Use the verb to make up a silly sentence about one person, place, or thing. Then use the same verb to make up a sentence about more than one person, place, or thing. Don't forget to add **s** when you need to!

TFK Tips for Writers

When you are writing about something that is happening now, check all the verbs. Be sure you have added **s** to verbs that tell about one person, place, or thing.

Verbs That Tell About the Past

Name _____ Date _____

A **verb** can tell about an action that happened in the past.

Add **ed** to most verbs to show that something happened in the past.

Now	In the Past
push	They **pushed** the boats to the water.
float	The boats **floated** across the finish line.
walk	We **walked** near one boat.

❶ Show What You Know

Finish each sentence. Change the verb in ( ) so that it tells about the past.

1. Families _____ the Olympics. (enjoy)

2. They _____ many sports. (watch)

3. Some runners _____ over high bars. (jump)

4. People _____ on a thin beam. (walk)

5. Many people _____ for their teams. (cheer)

Verbs That Tell About the Past

Name _____ Date _____

❷ Take It Up a Notch

Write a verb to finish each sentence. Add <u>ed</u> to a verb from the box.

| listen | sail | kick | play | enjoy |

1. Two teams _____ a game of soccer.

2. Simon _____ the ball toward the net.

3. The ball _____ high into the air.

4. The teams _____ to the cheers of the crowd.

5. We _____ the soccer game so much!

• •

❸ On Your Own

A Verb Hunt Go on a verb hunt! Look at a book you are reading. See how many past tense verbs you can find that end with **ed**. Write down as many as you can in five minutes. Then compare your list with a friend's list.

TFK Tips for Writers

You can make your writing clear by choosing verbs carefully. If you want readers to know that you are telling about something that already happened, be sure to use verbs that end in **ed**.

20 Grammar, Usage, and Mechanics—Level 2   #10127 (iz98)

Special Verbs

Name _____ Date _____

Special Verbs

The verbs **am, is,** and **are** tell about what is happening now. The verbs **was** and **were** tell about what happened in the past.

Use **am** with the word **I** in now sentences about yourself.

Use **is** or **was** to tell about one person, place, or thing.

Use **are** or **were** to tell about more than one person, place, or thing.

Now	In the Past
I **am** a beekeeper.	I **was** a beekeeper.
The honey **is** sweet.	The honey **was** sweet.
Those bees **are** busy.	Those bees **were** busy.

❶ Show What You Know

Circle the correct verb in ( ) to finish each sentence that happened in the past.

1. Mr. Scott (is/was) a beekeeper.

2. I (was/am) at his house.

3. His beehive (was/is) very big.

4. Thousands of bees (am/were) inside.

5. The bees (is/were) fun to watch.

Go on

Grammar, Usage, and Mechanics—Level 2

Special Verbs

Name _____ Date _____

❷ Take It Up a Notch

Write a verb from the box to finish each sentence.

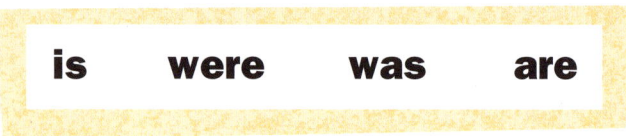

is   were   was   are

1. The bees _____ busy now.

2. I _____ near their hive before.

3. The bees _____ hard at work then.

4. Now their honey _____ ready to eat!

❸ On Your Own

Sentences for Bees Work with a partner to write the verbs **am, is, are, was,** and **were** on cards. Put the cards into a small bag or box. Take turns pulling out a card. Make up a sentence a bee might say that uses the verb on the card.

TFK Tips for Writers

Sometimes you may want to join two short sentences to make a longer, smooth sentence. If you do, be sure to change the verb when it tells about more than one.

Example: Josh **is** a beekeeper. Amy **is** a beekeeper.

Josh and Amy **are** beekeepers.

Other Special Verbs

Name _____ Date _____

Other Special Verbs

Most verbs that tell about the past end with **ed.** Some special verbs change their spelling when they tell about the past.

Now	In the Past
do, does	did
get, gets	got
have, has	had
make, makes	made

Now: Dad **gets** some mittens from the closet.
In the Past: Dad **got** some mittens from the closet.

Now: All the trees **have** snow on them.
In the Past: All the trees **had** snow on them.

❶ Show What You Know

Finish each sentence. Change the verb in ( ) so that it tells about the past.

1. Ara and I _____ a snowman. (make)

2. We _____ a great job! (do)

3. Then our cousins _____ a snowball fight. (have)

4. They _____ soaking wet. (get)

5. We all _____ fun outside. (have)

Other Special Verbs

Name _____ Date _____

❷ Take It Up a Notch

Write the past form of a verb from the box to finish each sentence.

| does | gets | make | has |

1. Molly _____ on the chair lift.

2. She _____ her snowboard with her.

3. Skiers _____ tracks in the snow.

4. Molly _____ a flip in the air!

❸ On Your Own

Snowball Verbs Play this game in groups of four. Each person should cut out a white paper circle. Then everyone should write a sentence that uses **do, get, have,** or **make** on his or her snowball. Put the snowballs face down on a table. Take turns choosing one. Say the sentence, changing the verb to tell about the past. If your sentence is correct, keep the snowball. See how many you can collect!

TFK Tips for Writers

What can you do if you don't know how to spell a verb that tells about the past? Use a dictionary! If a verb changes its spelling when it tells about the past, you'll find that spelling listed when you look up the verb that tells about now.

Contractions

A **contraction** is a short way of writing words.

In most contractions made with **not,** an apostrophe **'** takes the place of the letter **o.**

(are n<u>o</u>t) aren't	(is n<u>o</u>t) isn't
(do n<u>o</u>t) don't	(was n<u>o</u>t) wasn't
	(were n<u>o</u>t) weren't

In contractions made with **I,** an apostrophe **'** takes the place of one or two letters.

(I <u>a</u>m) I'm	(I <u>ha</u>ve) I've	(I <u>wi</u>ll) I'll

❶ Show What You Know

Write the words that the underlined contraction in each sentence stands for.

1. <u>I've</u> never been to a pet show before. _____

2. The judges <u>aren't</u> ready yet. _____

3. Soon <u>I'll</u> watch the dogs race. _____

4. I <u>don't</u> know which one will win. _____

Contractions

Name _____ Date _____

❷ Take It Up a Notch

Write the contraction for the underlined words in each sentence.

1. We <u>were not</u> going to give Bart a bath. _____

2. He <u>was not</u> very dirty this morning. _____

3. We <u>do not</u> know how Bart got so muddy. _____

4. Now <u>I am</u> rubbing soap on him. _____

5. Bart <u>is not</u> muddy any more! _____

 **Proofreading Power!**

Find six mistakes in this news story. Use proofreader's marks to fix them.

Last Saturday, the students haved a big pet show at Piggley Park. Many people was there. Cute dogs walkd around a ring. Then they jump through hoops. Some animals getted ribbons. Be sure you do'nt miss the show next year!

∧	Add
—	Take out
/	Make a lowercase letter
≡	Make a capital letter
⊙	Add a period

26 Grammar, Usage, and Mechanics—Level 2

Adjectives

An **adjective** is a describing word that tells how something looks, feels, sounds, tastes, or smells.

Look	We stopped at a **colorful** booth.
Feel	Dad bought me a **warm** pretzel.
Sound	I heard **loud** music playing.
Taste	Mom ate some **spicy** chicken.
Smell	I called it **stinky** chicken!

Adjectives can tell how something looks by describing size, shape, color, or how many.

Size	Shape	Color	How Many
huge	flat	blue	few
little	round	red	nine
tall	square	tan	some

❶ Show What You Know

Read each sentence. Circle the adjective that tells how something looks, feels, sounds, tastes, or smells.

1. Julia and I sat on the hard seat.
2. The ride started moving with a loud buzz.
3. We saw bright lights as the ride spun around.
4. The smell of fresh popcorn filled the air.
5. I could hardly wait to try a buttery bagful!

Go on

Adjectives

Name _____ Date _____

❷ Take It Up a Notch
Circle the adjective on each line that is the correct sense word to finish the paragraph.

I went into a huge/yummy tent. A soft/big
             ——————   ————
               look   look

man with a loud/stinky voice called me. He told
          —————————
            sound

me to pick up a smooth/tiny hoop. I tossed it onto
                ——————————
                  feel

a peg and won a small/hard, furry/sweet animal.
                —————————— ——————————
                  look   feel

Next, I bought a sweet/bumpy candied apple that
                 ——————————
                   taste

had a fresh/rough smell.
      ——————————
         smell

• •

❸ On Your Own
Adjective Riddles Describe an animal, a place, or a thing in a riddle. Use adjectives that tell how it looks, feels, sounds, tastes, and smells. For example, you might say, "I am a small, soft animal. I have sharp claws. I make a purring sound. What am I?" (Answer: a kitten). Take turns with a partner making up and answering the riddles.

TFK Tips for Writers

Does your writing sometimes sound flat and boring? Make your sentences come to life by using sense words to help your reader picture what you're describing.

Example: Luke's ˰sweet corn won a prize at the fair.

a, an, and *the*

Name _____ Date _____

a, an, and *the*

The words **a, an,** and **the** are adjectives.

Use **a** and **an** before nouns that name one person, place, or thing.

    Use **a** before words that begin with a consonant sound.

    Use **an** before words that begin with a vowel sound.

        Uncle Karl got on **a** ferry.

        It took him to **an** island.

• •

Use **the** before nouns that name one specific person, place, or thing, or more than one.

    Visitors looked up at **the** tall statue.

    They counted **the** points on her crown.

    They saw **the** torch in her hand.

• • • • • • • • • • • • • • • • • • •

❶ Show What You Know
Draw a line under the correct word in ( ).

1. (a/an) suitcase
2. (a/the) buses
3. (a/an) airport
4. (a/an) old car
5. (an/the) bumpy road
6. (a/an) map

Go on

a, an, and *the*

Name _____ Date _____

❷ Take It Up a Notch

Write the correct word in ( ) on the line to finish each sentence.

1. Mom had _____ idea. (a, an)

2. We would go on _____ trip to New York. (a, an)

3. We rode on _____ underground trains. (the, a)

4. I liked seeing _____ tall buildings. (a, the)

5. We went to see _____ play. (an, a)

• •

❸ On Your Own

Pack Your Bags! Play a memory game with a group. One player says, "I'm going on a trip, and in my suitcase I will pack [a/an noun]." (Example: I will pack an apple.) Each player repeats <u>in order</u> every item packed so far, and then adds a new one. Players must use **a, an,** or **the** before each noun. They earn a point for using **a, an,** or **the** correctly and another point for naming every item in the suitcase.

TFK Tips for Writers

Proofread a paper you are writing to be sure you have used **an,** not **a,** before words that begin with a vowel sound.

Special Adjectives

Special Adjectives

Some describing words are made from the names of places. These **special adjectives** begin with capital letters.

Place Names	Special Adjectives
Africa	**African** desert
Alaska	**Alaskan** fish
China	**Chinese** silk
France	**French** bread
India	**Indian** dresses
Italy	**Italian** art
Mexico	**Mexican** maracas
Spain	**Spanish** dancers

Maracas make music.

❶ Show What You Know
Find and write the special adjective in each sentence.

1. Mei is my Chinese pen pal. _____

2. Our Spanish teacher plays tapes. _____

3. Jed loves Italian food! _____

4. Do you know any Mexican songs? _____

5. African elephants live in herds. _____

Special Adjectives

Name _____ Date _____

❷ Take It Up a Notch
Finish each sentence. Write a special adjective made from the place name in ( ).

1. Two _____ dogs pulled the sled. (Alaska)

2. We gave Nona _____ perfume. (France)

3. The _____ art showed waterfalls. (China)

4. Bombay is a large _____ city. (India)

❸ On Your Own
Around the World Get a globe or world map. On your own or with a partner, find and list the names of some countries. Beside each country's name, write the special adjective made from the name. See how many countries and special adjectives you can write. Use a dictionary to check your work.

TFK Tips for Writers

Special adjectives can come in handy when you're writing a story or a report. Try using them to make your writing flow better with fewer words.

                Mexican
Example: Tanya has a ∧ piñata ~~that came from Mexico~~.

Comparing with Adjectives

Name _____ Date _____

Adjectives sometimes tell how people, places, or things are alike or different.

Add **er** to adjectives to compare two people, places, or things.

The water in this lake is **colder** than the water in the ocean.

It is **cleaner** than the water in the frog pond.

Add **est** to adjectives to compare more than two people, places, or things.

This lake has the **coldest** water of all the lakes here.

Mirror Lake has the **cleanest** water I've ever seen.

❶ Show What You Know

Circle the correct adjective in ( ) to finish each sentence.

1. Kanika has the (newer/newest) fishing pole in the family.

2. It is (longer/longest) than my pole.

3. Our boat is (faster/fastest) than our friend's boat.

4. It is the (quieter/quietest) boat on the lake.

5. We like fishing where the water is (deeper/deepest) of all.

Comparing with Adjectives

Name _____ Date _____

❷ Take It Up a Notch

Finish each sentence. Add <u>er</u> or <u>est</u> to the adjective in ( ).

1. Today is the _____ day of the week. (bright)

2. The sun feels _____ at the lake than at home. (warm)

3. The air smells _____ here than in the city. (fresh)

4. That tree is the _____ I've ever seen. (tall)

5. It is _____ than I am! (old)

✓ Proofreading Power!

Find five mistakes in these sentences from a journal. Use proofreader's marks to fix them.

July 22

Dad and I walked down to the lake this morning. Our german shepherd, Penny, came with us. She barked at an american bald eagle that we saw flying above us.

Later we picked some wild berries growing near a old elm tree. They were more smaller this summer than last year. But they were the sweeter berries I ever tasted!

∧	Add
—	Take out
/	Make a lowercase letter
≡	Make a capital letter
⊙	Add a period

34   Grammar, Usage, and Mechanics—Level 2

Adverbs That Tell How

Name _____ Date _____

Adverbs That Tell How

An **adverb** is a describing word that can tell how an action is done. Many adverbs end with **ly.**

A seagull glided **gracefully** above us.

It flew **silently** to the rocky cliffs.

It waited **calmly** for other seagulls.

More seagulls arrived **quickly.**

❶ Show What You Know
Draw a line under the adverb in each sentence.

1. The rocket rose noisily.

2. It quickly flew into space.

3. Scientists carefully checked their instruments.

4. The astronauts silently watched the earth below them.

5. The next week, the shuttle landed safely in the desert.

Adverbs That Tell How

Name _____ Date _____

❷ Take It Up a Notch
Make the underlined word an adverb by adding ly.

1. Inez <u>proud</u>_____ showed Jan the kite she worked hard to make.

2. Then she <u>firm</u>_____ attached a long piece of string.

3. Holding the kite up, she ran <u>swift</u>_____ down the hill.

4. The kite <u>silent</u>_____ flew above her.

5. A gentle breeze <u>slow</u>_____ lifted it higher and higher.

❸ On Your Own
How Do You Do That? With a partner, think of three adverbs. Write them in a row on a piece of paper. Below each adverb, list actions that go with the adverb. For example, ask yourself, "What do I do carefully? What do I do quietly?" See how many actions you can think of that go with each adverb.

TFK Tips for Writers

Good writers use adverbs to describe exactly how something happened. Look at a story you are writing. See if you can add some adverbs to paint a clearer word picture.

Example: The pilot ^calmly landed the jet.

Adverbs That Tell When or Where

Some adverbs describe when or where an action happens.

When	Many stars are shining **now.** The boys **sometimes** look for shooting stars. **Soon** a full moon will appear.
Where	Plants and animals live **here** on Earth. I can see them **everywhere!** Look **up** and see the moon.

❶ Show What You Know

Write <u>when</u> or <u>where</u> to tell what each underlined adverb describes.

1. We stand <u>here</u> at night. _____

2. Everyone looks <u>up</u>. _____

3. I <u>sometimes</u> see something new! _____

4. <u>Now</u> I found the Dog Star. _____

5. I wonder what I will spot <u>soon</u>! _____

Adverbs That Tell When or Where

Name _____   Date _____

❷ Take It Up a Notch

Draw a line under the adverb in each sentence.

1. The night sky often changes.
2. Sometimes we can see planets.
3. Lara looks at Mars today.
4. A robot has landed there.
5. It moves forward on wheels.

 **Proofreading Power!**

Find four mistakes in this e-mail message. Use proofreader's marks to fix them.

Hi Jake!

   I am sorry that you missed our trip to the science museum tomorrow. It was really fun. The man who showed us the rockets and space suits spoke loud so everyone could hear. I could see clear even from the back of the room. His talk about the moon rocks went by quickly. Feel better soonly.

∧	Add
—	Take out
/	Make a lowercase letter
≡	Make a capital letter
⊙	Add a period

38   Grammar, Usage, and Mechanics—Level 2

Pronouns

A **pronoun** is a naming word that can take the place of one or more nouns. **I** is the pronoun you use to talk about yourself. Use other pronouns to take the place of other nouns.

Nouns	Pronouns
<u>Pedro</u> likes games.	**He** likes games.
<u>Hayley</u> plays checkers.	**She** plays checkers.
<u>That game</u> is fun.	**It** is fun.
<u>Sia and I</u> hide.	**We** hide.
<u>Gen and Ping</u> won.	**They** won.

❶ Show What You Know

Circle the pronoun in ( ) that can take the place of the underlined word or words in each sentence.

1. <u>Suzi and I</u> stand on one side of the net. (She/We)

2. <u>Ken and Jack</u> stand on the other side of the net. (They/He)

3. <u>Ken</u> passes the ball to Jack. (They/He)

4. <u>The ball</u> soars over the net. (They/It)

Go on ➡

Grammar, Usage, and Mechanics—Level 2   39

Pronouns

Name _____ Date _____

❷ Take It Up a Notch

Write the pronoun that can take the place of the underlined word or words.

| He | She | It | They |

1. The children play computer games. _____

2. Liz clicks on a frog. _____

3. The frog hops across the screen. _____

4. Greg keeps track of the score. _____

❸ On Your Own

Quiz Kids Put on your own quiz show! Each player should write three questions about different topics. Put the questions in a bag. Take turns pulling out a question and answering it. Begin each answer with a pronoun. Earn one point for using the right pronoun. Earn another point for giving the correct answer.

Example: What do clocks tell us?

Answer: They tell us the time.

TFK Tips for Writers

When you use pronouns, be sure it is clear which noun the pronoun is naming. In the second sentence, readers won't know who **He** is: "Bud and Abe went shopping. He got a game."

More Pronouns

Some pronouns are used in the **naming part** of a sentence.

Jim goes to a cooking school.

He goes to a cooking school.

Other pronouns are used in the **action part** of a sentence.

The teacher shows **him** how to add.

Mrs. Holt asked **her** to practice.

The principal gives **us** our spelling words.

The children try to remember **them.**

❶ Show What You Know

Write the correct pronoun on the line to finish each sentence.

1. Mr. Chen teaches _____ . (we/us)

2. He tells _____ about dinosaurs. (us/we)

3. Ella is writing about _____ . (they/them)

4. Mr. Chen gave _____ some books. (she/her)

More Pronouns

Name _____ Date _____

❷ Take It Up a Notch

Write the correct pronoun to finish the second sentence in each pair.

1. Firefighters go to school, too! Going to school helps _____ do their jobs better.

2. Everyone practices using hoses. Firefighters need _____ to spray water on fires.

3. Some men learn to climb a building. They take a dog with _____ to help search inside.

4. Rita teaches ways to stop forest fires. The students learn from _____ what to do.

 **Proofreading Power!**

Find four mistakes in this paragraph. Use proofreader's marks to fix them.

Can we go to the library tomorrow? Us are learning about Dr. Seuss. I want to find some books written by them. Mrs. Rossi asked we to bring one book to school. Us will read our favorite part to the class.

∧	Add
—	Take out
/	Make a lowercase letter
≡	Make a capital letter
⊙	Add a period

Possessive Nouns

Name _____ Date _____

Possessive Nouns

A noun can show that a person or an animal owns or has something.

When a noun names one person, place, or thing, add **'s** to show ownership.

Grandma's scrapbook is filled with pictures.

Do you like the picture of her **dog's** puppies?

That **puppy's** tail is wagging!

Emily's friend will like these pictures.

• •

❶ **Show What You Know**

Write each underlined word correctly so that it shows ownership.

1. Aunt <u>Lian</u> camera   _____

2. one <u>dog</u> tail   _____

3. my <u>mother</u> glasses   _____

4. <u>Kofi</u> pictures   _____

5. the <u>team</u> coach   _____

Grammar, Usage, and Mechanics—Level 2

Possessive Nouns

Name _____ Date _____

❷ Take It Up a Notch
Finish each sentence. Make the noun in red show ownership.

1. My _____ hobby is taking pictures.
   _{sister}

2. She snaps shots all over our _____ house.
   _{family}

3. Some pictures are of our _____ kittens.
   _{cat}

4. One shows our _____ floppy ears.
   _{rabbit}

5. The best pictures are of _____ messy room!
   _{Ned}

❸ On Your Own
A Family Portrait Draw a picture of your family, including pets. Add name labels. Show each person and animal with something he or she really likes. (Someone who plays soccer might hold a soccer ball.) Then trade papers with a friend. Have your friend name things in your picture, using nouns that show ownership.

Example: Diego's soccer ball

TFK Tips for Writers

Look for places in your writing where a noun that shows ownership can shorten your writing and make it flow better.

Example: The ^clown's bike ~~that belongs to the clown~~ has only one wheel!

44 Grammar, Usage, and Mechanics—Level 2

More Possessive Nouns

A noun can show that two or more people or animals own or have something.

When a noun names more than one person, place, or thing, add **s'** to show ownership.

All the **tumblers'** sneakers are red.

Those **tigers'** teeth look sharp!

The **clowns'** tricks are funny.

❶ Show What You Know

Write each underlined word correctly so that it shows ownership by more than one.

1. these <u>elephants</u> trunks   _____

2. both <u>horses</u> saddles   _____

3. all the <u>trainers</u> animals   _____

4. some <u>parents</u> tickets   _____

5. three <u>lions</u> manes   _____

More Possessive Nouns

Name _____ Date _____

❷ Take It Up a Notch

Circle the noun in ( ) that shows ownership of more than one.

1. Both (boy's/boys') faces looked happy.

2. The two (clown's/clowns') tiny bikes were funny.

3. Some (juggler's/jugglers') pins twirled in the air.

4. All the (girl's/girls') costumes sparkled.

5. Those (seal's/seals') tricks made us laugh!

❸ On Your Own

The Circus Life There are lots of jobs to do at the circus. Pretend that you are in charge. Make a list of jobs you want the workers to do. Each job on your list should have a noun that names more than one and shows ownership. For example, you might write "clean the lions' cages." See what circus jobs you can add to the list!

TFK Tips for Writers

Look for places in your writing where a noun shows ownership. Does the noun name one person, place, or thing, or does it name more than one? Make sure you have put the apostrophe in the right spot!

When the noun names one:
The announcer**'s** coat is black.

When the noun names more than one:
The announcer**s'** coats are black.

Possessive Pronouns

Name _____ Date _____

Possessive Pronouns

You know that some nouns show that a person or an animal owns or has something. Some pronouns can also show ownership.

Pronouns That Show Ownership						
my	your	her	his	its	our	their

Pronouns that show ownership can take the place of nouns that show ownership.

The girls' parrots can talk.   **Their** parrots can talk.

Becca's parrot says, "Hello!"   **Her** parrot says, "Hello!"

Mac's dog cannot talk.   **His** dog cannot talk.

The dog's bark is loud.   **Its** bark is loud.

❶ Show What You Know
Draw a line under each pronoun that shows ownership.

1. My family likes to watch birds.

2. Dad, Paul, and I look for birds behind our house.

3. "Don't forget your bird book!" Dad says.

4. When I see a bird, I look in the book to find its name.

5. Then I read about where the birds build their nests.

Grammar, Usage, and Mechanics—Level 2

Possessive Pronouns

Name _____ Date _____

❷ Take It Up a Notch

Write the pronoun that could take the place of the underlined word or words.

| Her | Their | His | Its |

1. Dan's sister Dara spots a hummingbird. _____

2. The bird's feathers are tiny. _____

3. Dan's and Dara's bird feeders are full. _____

4. Dara's tasty birdseed is good! _____

Proofreading Power!

Find four mistakes in these sentences from a report. Use proofreader's marks to fix them.

Birds have feathers, a beak, and wings. They have no teeth. Bird's bones can be hollow. Birds have a strong heart. A small bird's heart beats more quickly than ours hearts do. A persons heart will beat only about 60 to 90 times in a minute. A hummingbirds' heart can beat 1,000 times a minute!

∧	Add
—	Take out
/	Make a lowercase letter
≡	Make a capital letter
⊙	Add a period

Capitalization and Punctuation Guide

Name _____ Date _____

Days and Months

The names of the seven days of the week are special nouns. These names begin with capital letters.

Sunday	**M**onday	**T**uesday	**W**ednesday
Thursday	**F**riday	**S**aturday	

The names of the twelve months of the year are special nouns, too. These names begin with capital letters.

January	**F**ebruary	**M**arch	**A**pril
May	**J**une	**J**uly	**A**ugust
September	**O**ctober	**N**ovember	**D**ecember

The names of the days and the months begin with capital letters, even when they are used in sentences.

On **Wednesday,** we went bowling.

We went bowling again on **Sunday.**

I learned to bowl in **December.**

My score was 150 in **March.**

Grammar, Usage, and Mechanics—Level 2

Capitalization and Punctuation Guide

Name _____ Date _____

❶ Show What You Know

Find the names of the days and the months in each line. Circle the letters that should be capital letters.

1. Our nature club meets every monday afternoon.

2. In september, we take a lot of nature walks.

3. We collect leaves and make a leaf book in november.

4. In june, we look for wildflowers.

5. Each member draws in a nature journal on fridays.

Proofreading Power!

Find four mistakes in this list. Use proofreader's marks to fix them.

The Bookworm Book Club

Monday, march 14

Meet at Nick's house at three o'clock.

Thursday, April 28

Make bookmarks to give away at the library next saturday.

tuesday, May 17

Choose a book to read together in june.

Decide if we will have a meeting in July.

∧	Add
—	Take out
/	Make a lowercase letter
≡	Make a capital letter
⊙	Add a period

Capitalization and Punctuation Guide

Name _____   Date _____

Abbreviations and Titles

An **abbreviation** is a short way of writing one or more words. An abbreviation often begins with a capital letter and ends with a period.

You can use an abbreviation when you write a street name.

Street Name	Abbreviation
Park Avenue	Park **Ave.**
Windy Lane	Windy **Ln.**

Street Name	Abbreviation
Glen Road	Glen **Rd.**
Main Street	Main **St.**

You can use an abbreviation for the names of some months. **May, June,** and **July** are short names. They do not need abbreviations.

Month	Abbreviation
January	**Jan.**
February	**Feb.**
March	**Mar.**
April	**Apr.**
August	**Aug.**

Month	Abbreviation
September	**Sept.**
October	**Oct.**
November	**Nov.**
December	**Dec.**

A title before a person's name is usually written as an abbreviation. The title **Miss** is not an abbreviation.

Title	When to Use
Dr.	for a doctor
Miss	for a young woman
Mr.	for any man
Mrs.	for a married woman
Ms.	for any woman

Grammar, Usage, and Mechanics—Level 2   **51**

Capitalization and Punctuation Guide

Name _____ Date _____

① **Show What You Know**

Write each title or abbreviation correctly.

1. Lake ave   _____
2. Mr John Roberts   _____
3. feb   _____
4. Grove st.   _____
5. mrs Bess Larson   _____

 **Proofreading Power!**

Find six mistakes on this postcard. Use proofreader's marks to fix them.

Dear Aunt Clara,   aug 15

　We are having a great time on vacation! The Sea st. beach is beautiful. Dad's friend dr Moss took us sailing.

　Please come and visit us in september!

　　　　　Love,
　　　　　Mario

Mrs. Clara Ramos
42 Peach Tree Ln.
Atlanta, GA 30303

∧ Add	≡ Make a capital letter
— Take out	⊙ Add a period
/ Make a lowercase letter	

Capitalization and Punctuation Guide

Name _____ Date _____

Commas

Use a comma between the day and the year in a date.

> Mayor Sparks gave a speech on May 10, 2002.
>
> Mom and Dad voted on November 2, 2004.

A series is a list of three or more things. Use a comma between each thing on the list. There should be a comma after every item except the last one.

> The election would decide who would be the mayor, the governor, and the president.
>
> Mom, Dad, and I went to the voting place.

Use a comma between the name of a city and the name of a state.

> We met the President in Columbus, Ohio.
>
> Which presidents went to school in Princeton, New Jersey?
>
> Did any presidents grow up in Boston, Massachusetts?

Capitalization and Punctuation Guide

Name _____   Date _____

❶ Show What You Know

Put commas where they belong on each line.

1. March 15 1999
2. Fairbanks Alaska
3. October 23 2005
4. Portland Maine
5. coat tie and beard

Abraham Lincoln

Proofreading Power!

Find four mistakes in this list. Use proofreader's marks to fix them.

Presidents	Birthdays
John Adams was born in Braintree Massachusetts.	October 30, 1735
Abraham Lincoln was born in Hardin County, Kentucky.	February 12 1809
Franklin Roosevelt was born in Hyde Park New York.	January 30 1882

Proofreader's marks:
- ∧ Add
- — Take out
- / Make a lowercase letter
- ≡ Make a capital letter
- ⊙ Add a period

Quotation Marks

Use quotation marks " " in sentences that tell what someone says.

- Put the quotation marks before and after the exact words of the speaker. Be sure to write the second quotation mark after the end mark.

- Start a quotation with a capital letter. Use a comma or another kind of end mark between the quotation and the words that tell who is speaking.

> Tyler asked, "Have you been on a whale watch before?"
> Ross said, "This is the first one."

> "Look over there!" Tyler shouted.
> "Can all whales jump like that?" Ross asked.

Capitalization and Punctuation Guide

Name _____ Date _____

❶ Show What You Know

Add the missing quotation marks to these sentences.

1. Nyla asked, Where do whales live?
2. They live in the ocean, said Cleo.
3. Nyla asked, Are whales fish?
4. Cleo answered, No, whales are mammals.
5. They breathe air and are warm-blooded, she added.

✓ Proofreading Power!

Find five mistakes in these sentences from an interview. Use proofreader's marks to fix them.

Zack asked, What kind of whales do you study?"

Mr. Harris answered, "I study huge blue whales.

Zack asked, How big is an adult blue whale?

Mr. Harris said, It is larger than the biggest dinosaur!"

∧	Add
—	Take out
/	Make a lowercase letter
=	Make a capital letter
⊙	Add a period

Usage Guide

Name _____ Date _____

Using *I* and *me*

I or *me*

You use the pronouns **I** and **me** when you talk about yourself.

To tell which word to use, try saying a sentence with **I** and **me.** See which word sounds right.

Right: **I** spent all day swimming.
Wrong: **Me** spent all day swimming.

Right: Then Mom took **me** home.
Wrong: Then Mom took **I** home.

Naming Yourself Last

Name yourself last when you talk about another person and yourself.

Sandy and **I** spent all day swimming at the beach.

Then Mom took Sandy and **me** home.

Name yourself last when you talk about more than one other person and yourself.

Mom, Sandy, and **I** had fun during the car ride home.

My dog was in the car with Mom, Sandy, and **me.**

Usage Guide

Name _____ Date _____

1 Show What You Know

Finish each sentence by adding I or me.

1. Sandy and _____ want to swim again.

2. She and _____ might go next week.

3. Sandy's mom can take Sandy and _____ .

4. Maybe our friend Joan can come with Sandy and _____ .

5. I hope Sandy, Joan, and _____ can go to the beach.

Proofreading Power!

Find four mistakes in this letter. Use proofreader's marks to fix them.

Hi Joan,

　　Sandy and me want you to go with us when we swim on Wednesday. If you can go, then Sandy and me will pick you up at two o'clock. You, Sandy, and me will have such fun! Let Sandy and I know if you can make it.

　　　　　　　　　Your friend,
　　　　　　　　　Dee

∧	Add
—	Take out
/	Make a lowercase letter
≡	Make a capital letter
⊙	Add a period

Combining Sentences

To make two sentences into one sentence, you can use the word **and.**

> I am traveling to Venus in my mind.
> I am taking a rocket ship.
> → I am traveling to Venus in my mind, **and** I am taking a rocket ship.

> I want to find out about rocks on Venus.
> I will be doing science tests.
> → I want to find out about Venus rocks, **and** I will be doing science tests.

- - -

To make two sentences into one sentence, you can also use the word **but.**

> It will be fun to visit Venus.
> I will come home in two weeks.
> → It will be fun to visit Venus, **but** I will come home in two weeks.

> I like Venus.
> I like Earth, too.
> → I like Venus, **but** I like Earth, too.

Remember to put a comma before **and** or **but** when you combine sentences.

Usage Guide

Name _____ Date _____

❶ Show What You Know

Add a comma on the first line. Add the connecting word and or but on the second line to combine the sentences.

1. Venus is Earth's closest planet neighbor ____ _____ it is very different from Earth.

2. Venus is about the same size as Earth ____ _____ it is much hotter than Earth.

3. Venus's air is very thick ____ _____ we think it has clouds that smell like rotten eggs.

4. People on Earth may wish they could travel to Venus ____ _____ that is not possible now.

✓ Proofreading Power!

Find three mistakes in this paragraph. Use proofreader's marks to fix them.

> We cannot send people to Venus. but there have been missions that have gone there without people. Spaceships have been sent to Venus. Machines we sent have given us information and they have even taken photos. We learn more as new missions happen but there is still lots more to find out.

Mark	Meaning
∧	Add
—	Take out
/	Make a lowercase letter
≡	Make a capital letter
⊙	Add a period